KIDNEY CANCER

Current and Emerging Trends
in Detection and Treatment

LINDA BICKERSTAFF

ROSEN
PUBLISHING®
New York

This book is dedicated to Lavern and John,
friends who have faced kidney cancer and come out fighting!

Published in 2012 by The Rosen Publishing Group, Inc.
29 East 21st Street, New York, NY 10010

Library of Congress Cataloging-in-Publication Data

Bickerstaff, Linda.
Kidney cancer: current and emerging trends in detection and treatment / Linda Bickerstaff.—1st ed.
    p. cm.—(Cancer and modern science)
Includes bibliographical references and index.
ISBN 978-1-4488-1309-4 (lib. bdg.)
1. Kidneys—Cancer—Juvenile literature. I. Title.
RC280.K5B53 2012
616.99'461—dc22

2010009844

Manufactured in the United States of America

CPSIA Compliance Information: Batch #S11YA: For further information, contact Rosen Publishing, New York, New York, at 1-800-237-9932.

On the cover: This renal cell carcinoma, magnified 1,300 times by a colored scanning electron microscope, is shown sending threadlike projections of cytoplasm into surrounding normal kidney tissue.

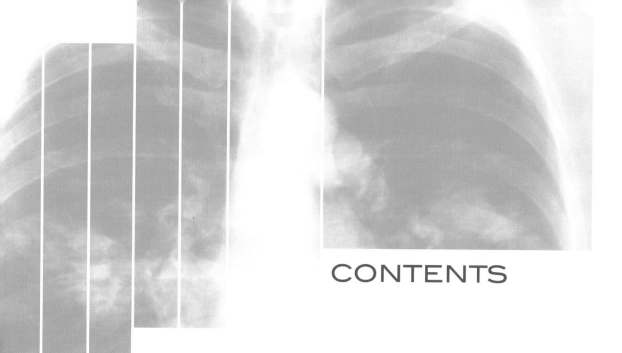

CONTENTS

INTRODUCTION

The kidneys are paired organs. They are the most important structures in the urinary system, which is one of the twelve organ systems found in the human body. The kidneys are responsible for regulating the amount of water that people have in their bodies. They also help eliminate waste materials that are made in various parts of the body. These waste materials are carried to the kidneys through the bloodstream.

Cancers can arise in the kidneys just as they can in any other organ in the body. According to the National Cancer Institute (NCI), the federal government's principal agency for cancer research and training, eleven million U.S. citizens are presently living with cancer. Of those people, 3 percent have kidney cancer. The NCI also estimates that between fifty thousand and sixty thousand people are diagnosed with kidney cancer each year. It is the cause of death in as many as thirteen thousand people yearly.

Kidney cancer rarely occurs in children or teens. Seventy-five percent of kidney cancers occur in adults over the age of fifty-five. Only

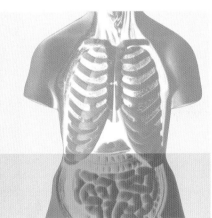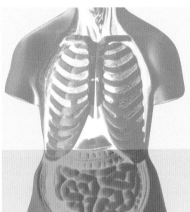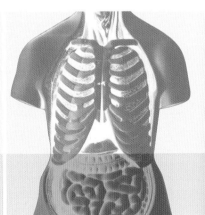

Haley Mathias is shown opening cards and packages on her twelfth birthday, two years after being diagnosed with a rare kind of kidney cancer called Wilms tumor. Ninety percent of children with Wilms tumor can be cured of their kidney cancers.

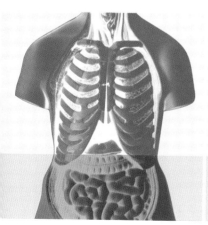
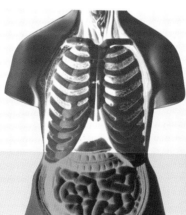
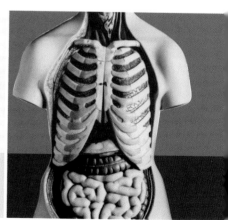

1.3 percent of kidney cancers occur in people under the age of twenty. The most common type of kidney cancer in young people is Wilms tumor. Almost all Wilms tumors are found in children who are six years old or younger, although this type of cancer can occasionally occur in teens and young adults. Because the majority of Wilms tumors are curable, there are many teens living today who are kidney cancer survivors.

After a brief review of the structure and function of the kidneys, this book will look at kidney cancer in detail. The goal of the book is to answer a few basic questions about kidney cancer: What causes it? Who gets it and why? Do children and teens need to worry about this type of cancer? How is it treated? Are new forms of treatment being developed? Is there anything a person can do to avoid getting kidney cancer? By learning the answers to these questions, readers can gain a better understanding of kidney cancer.

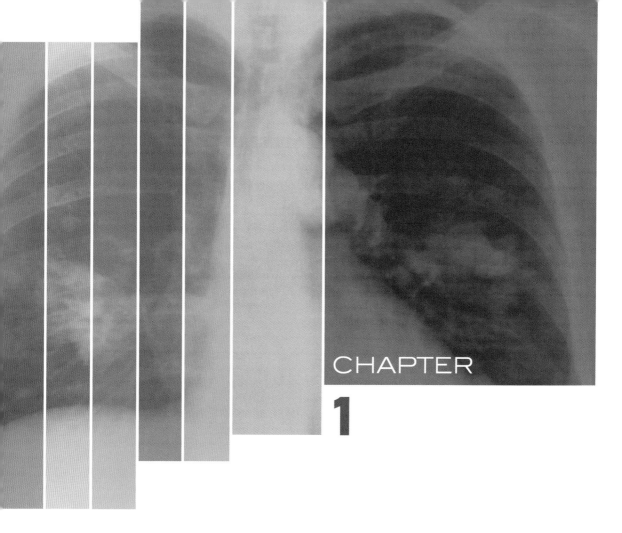

THE KIDNEYS: THE FACTS

The kidneys, along with their attached ureters, urinary bladder, urethra, and various glands, make up the urinary system of the body. The word "renal" is often used when talking about the kidneys. It comes from the Latin word for kidney and is used in identifying anything that relates to the kidneys.

Claudius Galen (129–216 CE), a Greek physician and anatomist, was probably the first person to recognize that the kidneys make urine. Leonardo da Vinci (1452–1519), an Italian artist, inventor, and

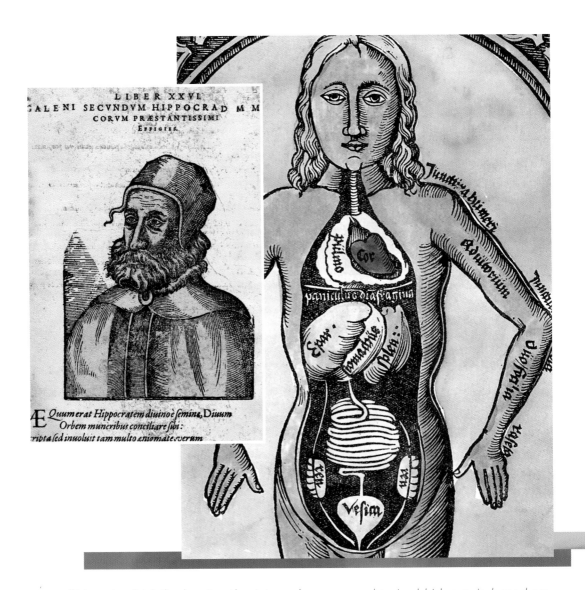

This print (right), showing the internal organs and paired kidneys, is based on the writings of Claudius Galen (129–216 CE), a Greek doctor and expert on the anatomy. Galen, who is pictured at left, was the first to associate the kidneys with the production of urine.

scientist, made detailed drawings of the parts of the urinary system in 1509. In the early years of the seventeenth century, three eyeglass makers invented an instrument that was the forerunner of the microscope. Dutch naturalist Antoni van Leeuwenhoek (1632–1723) improved this early instrument. He is credited with developing the modern microscope. Anatomists were soon looking at kidney tissue under the microscope. What they found was an organ made mainly of blood vessels and small tubes that wrapped around one another in intricate ways. It was the job of early physiologists to figure out how all the intricate parts of the kidneys worked together. How did the water that was a component of blood eventually end up as urine pouring out of the kidneys? They soon realized that the kidney was a very complex organ. Finding out how it actually worked was going to be a big job. The job was so big that a branch of medical science devoted to studying the kidney and its functions, called nephrology, was established in 1960. Nephrologists (doctors who take care of people with kidney problems) are still making new discoveries about the kidney and how it works.

Before looking at kidney cancer, it will be helpful to look at the structure of the kidneys and how they work.

RENAL ANATOMY

Most people are born with two kidneys. The right kidney is located on the right side of the spinal column just beneath the liver. The left kidney sits to the left of the spine beneath the spleen.

In adults, the kidneys are about 4 inches (10.2 centimeters) long and 1.5 inches (3.8 cm) wide. They are oval in shape. They have an indentation called the hilum on one side, which makes them look like the bean that bears their name, the kidney bean. This is the site where the renal artery and renal vein attach to the kidney. Blood from the heart is carried to the kidneys through the renal arteries, which branch directly off of the descending aorta. The aorta is the main artery responsible for carrying oxygenated blood away from the heart to the rest of the body. Blood from the kidneys returns to the heart through the renal veins. These veins attach to the inferior vena cava, the large vein that carries blood back to the heart from the lower body. The ureters, the tubes that carry urine from the kidneys to the urinary bladder, exit the kidneys near these blood vessels.

The part of the kidney that does most of the work is a microscopic structure called a nephron. There are approximately one million nephrons in each kidney. They are made up of a group of small tubes that wrap themselves around blood vessels. Water and waste materials that are filtered out of the blood by the nephrons eventually find their way into the renal pelvis. The renal pelvis is the funnel-shaped part of the kidney that attaches to the ureters.

RENAL PHYSIOLOGY

Renal physiology, or the functions of the kidney, involves the following four main jobs:

- The kidneys regulate the composition of a person's blood by either removing or reabsorbing small molecules and water from the bloodstream.
- They help control a person's blood pressure by making the enzyme renin.
- They produce erythropoietin, the hormone that stimulates the bone marrow to make red blood cells.
- They help adjust the amount of calcium present in a person's body.

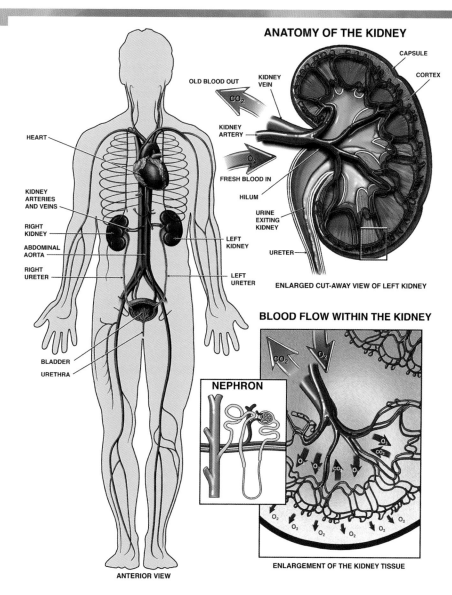

ANATOMY OF THE KIDNEY

CAPSULE

CORTEX

OLD BLOOD OUT

KIDNEY VEIN

CO₂

KIDNEY ARTERY

O₂

FRESH BLOOD IN

HILUM

URINE EXITING KIDNEY

URETER

ENLARGED CUT-AWAY VIEW OF LEFT KIDNEY

HEART

KIDNEY ARTERIES AND VEINS

RIGHT KIDNEY

ABDOMINAL AORTA

RIGHT URETER

LEFT KIDNEY

LEFT URETER

BLADDER

URETHRA

ANTERIOR VIEW

BLOOD FLOW WITHIN THE KIDNEY

CO₂

O₂

NEPHRON

O₂ CO₂

ENLARGEMENT OF THE KIDNEY TISSUE

This illustration shows the location of the kidneys, ureters, and bladder within the body. It also shows the complex anatomy of the kidney and the structure of a single nephron.

The parts of the kidney that are involved in the first of these jobs are its one million nephrons. Nephrons are the kidneys' filtering units. Twenty percent of the blood pumped away from the heart with each heartbeat goes into the kidneys and is carried to the nephrons. In the nephrons, water, waste materials such as urea, and ions such as sodium, potassium, and chloride are filtered out of the blood and into the small tubes of the nephrons. As the filtrate moves through the tubes, some of the water and most of the ions are reabsorbed back into the bloodstream. By the time the process is completed, a small amount of the water, most of the waste material, and only a few of the ions are left in the tubes. These substances form urine that then flows into the renal pelvis. From there, the urine moves out of the kidneys and into the ureters. All the blood in a person's body must pass through the kidneys at least twenty times each day to remove waste materials and keep the body's water content stable.

WATER, WATER EVERYWHERE

Although people may think that the human body seems pretty solid, 55 to 60 percent of the body is actually made of water. Two-thirds of the water in a person's body is found in his or her cells. The rest is found in the spaces surrounding cells or in the circulatory system. It is a major part of plasma, the liquid portion of blood. Excess water is filtered out of the body by the kidneys to keep the amount of water in body cells constant so that they can work properly. About 45 gallons (170 liters) of water are actually filtered out of a person's blood each day. All but 0.5 gallons (2 l) are reabsorbed to keep the total body water constant.

The kidneys help control a person's blood pressure by making an enzyme called renin. This enzyme is produced and stored in the cells of nephrons. Renin is one of several proteins that work together to control the amount of sodium present in the blood. If a person's blood pressure is too low, more renin is produced. This increased renin production results in more sodium and water being reabsorbed by the kidneys. When more sodium and water are reabsorbed, the volume of fluid circulating in the blood increases, and a person's blood pressure goes up.

Another substance that is produced in the kidneys is the hormone erythropoietin. This hormone travels from the kidneys to the bone marrow, where it triggers the production of red blood cells.

The fourth job of the kidney is to help regulate the amount of calcium in a person's body. It does this by converting vitamin D, which is made in the skin when it is exposed to sunlight, into a form that can be used to keep blood levels of calcium constant.

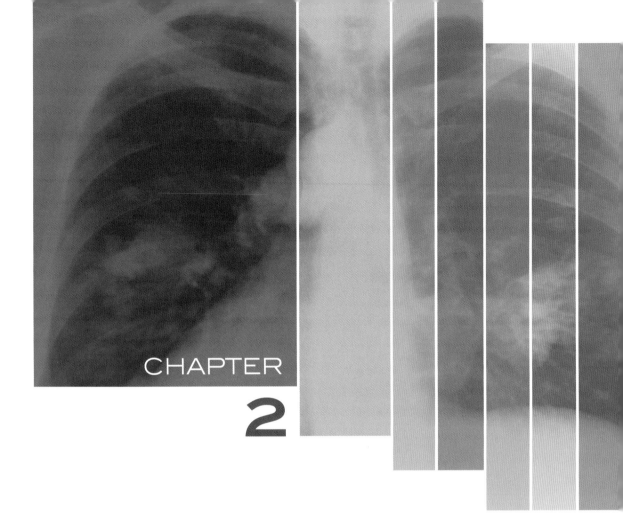

CANCER AND ITS CAUSES

Scientists at the NCI have identified more than two hundred types of cancer in humans. Each type of cancer has its own unique characteristics. Some cancers grow very slowly, whereas others grow and spread at unbelievable rates. Many cancers make people feel sick or cause them to have pain, while others cause no symptoms. A few cancers are easily treated, while others don't respond to any type of treatment. In spite of these differences, cancers have one thing in common. Cancers develop if a person's body loses its ability to control how often cells duplicate themselves, how quickly they grow, and when they die.

*Robert Hooke (1635–1703)
used this microscope in his
studies. Hooke was the first
person to describe the billions
of boxlike structures that make
up tissues. He called these
structures cells.*

Cell Basics

English physicist and inventor
Robert Hooke (1635–1703) was
one of the scientists who worked with Antoni van Leeuwenhoek on the
development of the microscope. In 1665, while examining a thin slice of
cork to see how the microscope worked, he noticed that cork was
made of hundreds of boxlike structures. The structures reminded him
of the small rooms that house monks in a monastery. He named these
structures "cells" because that's what the monks called their rooms.

Humans are also constructed of building blocks called cells. Cells
are made of a thick, gooey substance called cytoplasm, which is contained within a thin membrane. Suspended in the cytoplasm of the cell
is its control center, the nucleus. The nucleus is surrounded by the
nuclear membrane. Instead of being filled with cytoplasm, however,
the nucleus is filled with a chemical compound called deoxyribonucleic
acid (DNA).

Craig Freudenrich, an author and professor at Duke University in
Durham, North Carolina, wrote an article about DNA. He noted, "Like
the one ring of power in Tolkien's *Lord of the Rings*, deoxyribonucleic
acid (DNA) is the master molecule of every cell." DNA contains all of

the information necessary to direct the production of new cells. It also directs the production of proteins that control how the body works. DNA is the material that makes individuals unique from one another.

DNA is arranged in paired bundles called chromosomes. Humans have twenty-three pairs of chromosomes. The DNA in one chromosome of the pair is inherited from a person's mother and the other from his or her father. Contained within each chromosome are tiny bits of DNA called genes. Humans have between twenty thousand and twenty-five thousand genes scattered along their chromosomes. Genes provide the blueprints that direct the construction of proteins that have very specific functions. For instance, a group of genes control the production of specific proteins that determine a person's hair color and eye color.

Genes also provide the information necessary to make proteins that control how often cells divide, how fast they grow, and when they die. There are two specific genes that do this. Proto-oncogenes control cell growth. Tumor suppressor genes control cell division and cell death. These genes work together so that as cells grow old and die, new cells are made to replace them. This process is done in a controlled, orderly manner.

Uncontrolled Cell Growth Forms Cancers

If a proto-oncogene is damaged in some way, it mutates, or changes, into a gene called an oncogene. This gene doesn't have the information necessary to make the proteins that control cell growth. As a result, cells can grow quickly and wildly. If tumor suppressor genes mutate, the checks and balances of a cell's system are lost, and the cell can grow and divide rapidly without dying. The result of either type of mutation is the formation of a mass of cells called a tumor. Some tumors rarely cause problems

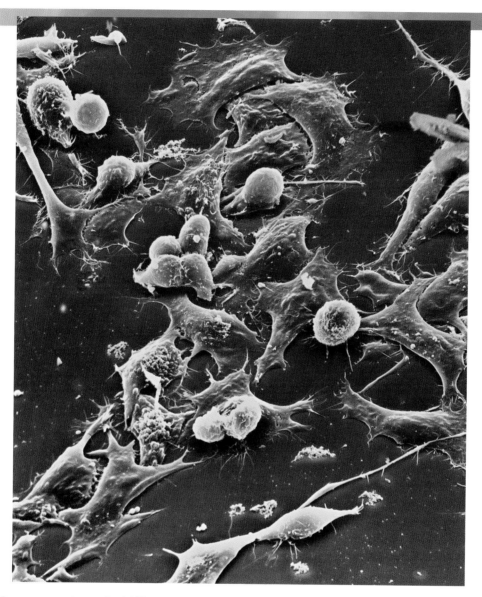

Cancers, such as the Wilms tumor pictured here, can develop if mutations occur to proto-oncogenes (which control cell growth) and tumor suppressor genes (which control cell division and death).

and are called benign tumors. Others cause many problems and can actually kill a person. These are called malignant tumors, or cancers.

CANCER, THE GREAT JIGSAW PUZZLE

Uncovering the secrets of cancer is like working a huge jigsaw puzzle. Since the time when cancer was first identified more than five thousand years ago, hundreds of thousands of people have slowly assembled pieces of the cancer jigsaw puzzle. It was slow going in the early years. As more puzzle pieces fell into place, however, a picture of cancer began to emerge. Today, scientists are adding pieces to the puzzle almost daily.

BUILDING THE BORDERS OF THE PUZZLE: THE EARLY YEARS

Cancer is not a modern disease. It was found in fossilized bones and in mummies buried in ancient Egyptian tombs. One of the first pieces of the cancer puzzle was placed by the founder of Egyptian medicine, Imhotep (2667–2648 BCE). He is credited with writing a work on the study of medicine. Many years later, remnants of his writing were discovered in seven ancient scrolls. Two of the seven scrolls mention growths that were probably cancers. The Edwin Smith Surgical Papyrus, from about 1600 BCE, is thought to be a copy of another of Imhotep's scrolls. It describes eight women who had large tumors of the breast that were undoubtedly malignant.

Several other puzzle pieces were placed by Hippocrates (460–370 BCE), a Greek physician. He created the word "cancer." Hippocrates thought that the blood vessels surrounding malignant tumors looked like the claws of a crab. He called these tumors *karkinos*, the Greek word for "crab." A Roman physician, Aulus Cornelius Celsus (25 BCE–50 CE), translated *karkinos* into the more familiar Latin word, "cancer."

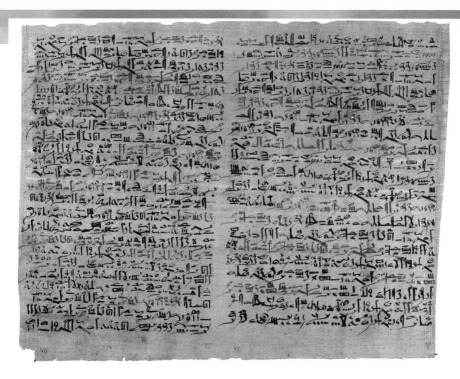

The Edwin Smith Surgical Papyrus, pictured here, is probably a copy of the work attributed to Imhotep (2667–2648 BCE), an Egyptian physician. It contains a description of breast cancer in eight women.

Hippocrates also proposed a theory about the cause of cancer. He believed that the human body contained four fluids, which he called humors. These controlled everything that happened in the body. The four humors were blood, phlegm, yellow bile, and black bile. According to his humoral theory of disease, a person who had too much black bile in his or her body would develop cancer. The humoral theory persisted for 1,900 years until the discovery of the lymphatic system in the seventeenth century by Italian physician Gaspare Aselli (1581–1626). He thought that abnormalities within the lymphatic system caused cancer.

THE STRUCTURE OF DNA

DNA is made up of only three substances: a sugar called deoxyribose, a phosphate group (phosphorus with an oxygen molecule attached to it), and a nitrogen-rich substance called a base. These three components form a nucleotide. There are four different bases (adenine, thymine, guanine, and cytosine), so there are four different nucleotides.

The structure of DNA, which American geneticist James Watson and British physicist Francis Crick described in 1953, resembles a spiral staircase. The handrails of the staircase are made of ribbons of deoxyribose molecules. Attached to each sugar molecule is a phosphate group. The two handrails are held together by the steps between them. Each step is made of two bases, called a base pair. These pairings are very specific. Adenine will only attach to thymine to form one base pair, while guanine will only attach to cytosine to form the other base pair. The entire structure curves around like a spiral staircase, giving DNA its distinctive double helix shape.

If all the pieces of DNA in a human cell were attached, the strand of DNA would be 6 feet (2 meters) long. Thanks to the Human Genome Project, scientists now know that all of the DNA in a human cell contains slightly more than three billion nucleotides with their three billion base pairs.

Many more puzzle pieces were added after Antoni van Leewenhoek invented the microscope and Robert Hooke discovered cells. Using the microscope, Johannes Müller (1801–1858), a German pathologist, recognized that cancers were made of cells and not lymph (although there are some cancers of the lymph system). This discovery ended the one-hundred-year reign of the lymph theory of cancer. Soon scientists were placing puzzle pieces at a rapid pace as knowledge about cells and their association with cancer multiplied.

Filling in the Puzzle: DNA and the Human Genome Project

By the middle of the nineteenth century it was evident that something in the nucleus of cells was critical to the functioning of cells and ultimately to the formation of cancers. That "something" was DNA. James Watson (1928–), an American geneticist, and Francis Crick (1916–2004), a British physicist, identified the structure of DNA in 1953. Their great discovery, however, was made possible by all of the puzzle pieces that had been supplied by the researchers who preceded them.

Once the structure of DNA was identified, huge numbers of puzzle pieces fell into place. The discovery opened the door for one of the most incredible accomplishments of modern science—the mapping of the entire human genome. In 1990, the Human Genome Project was begun under the direction of James Watson. More than a thousand scientists from around the world participated in the project. Each scientist, or group of scientists, was given a chunk of DNA from one of the chromosomes of a human cell to examine. The scientists counted the number and location of every base pair within the piece of DNA they received. The information from each scientist was then computerized and combined with the information from the other scientists. The

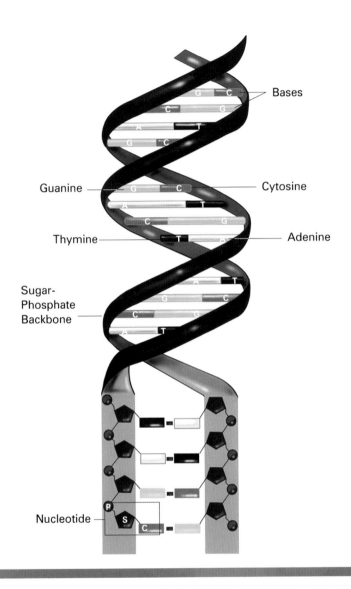

Bases

Guanine

Cytosine

Thymine

Adenine

Sugar-
Phosphate
Backbone

Nucleotide

James Watson (1928–) and Francis Crick (1916–2004) identified the structure of deoxyribonucleic acid (DNA) in 1953. This diagram clearly shows the spiral-ladder structure of DNA. It also shows the pairings of the bases that form the ladder's rungs: adenine and thymine, guanine and cytosine.

project was completed in 2003, much more quickly than originally pro-
jected. A map of the entire human genome had been made.

Among other things, the Human Genome Project identified
between twenty thousand and twenty-five thousand genes. The exact
location of these genes on the twenty-three paired chromosomes is
now known. Many gene mutations have already been identified, and
more are being discovered every day. Specific gene mutations that
cause some types of kidney cancer, for instance, have been identified.
This knowledge is being used to develop new ways to diagnose these
cancers at early stages so that they can be treated more successfully.
It is also being used to develop new drugs and other treatment methods to improve cancer survival.

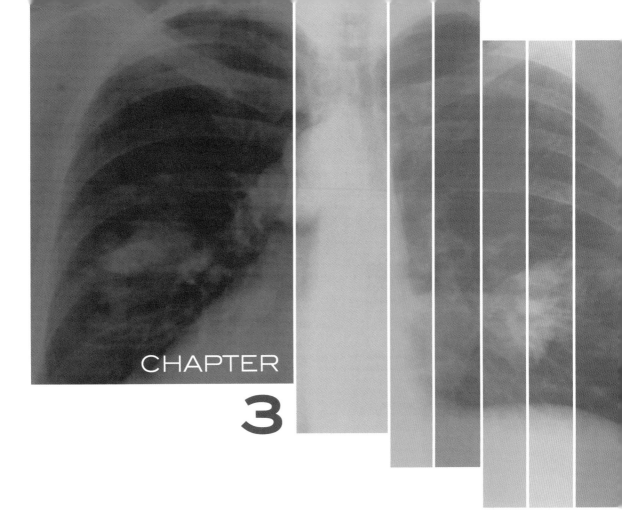

DIAGNOSING KIDNEY CANCER: A MEDICAL SCAVENGER HUNT

Scavenger hunts are very popular in the United States. Many teens organize them to raise money for various projects. Even television networks have developed programs such as *The Amazing Race* based on the idea of a scavenger hunt. In a scavenger hunt, people are given an initial set of clues. They then use the clues to follow leads to the next set of clues. When all the clues have been found, the hunt ends, and someone wins a prize. Medical scavenger hunts occur on a daily basis.

Instead of being called a scavenger hunt, however, the process is called "making a diagnosis." After a review of the various types of kidney cancer, a medical scavenger hunt will be undertaken to see how kidney cancers are diagnosed.

TYPES OF KIDNEY CANCER

The most common types of adult kidney cancer are renal cell carcinoma, transitional cell carcinoma, and renal sarcoma. In children, kidney cancers include Wilms tumor, mesoblastic nephromas, clear cell sarcomas, and rhabdoid tumors of the kidney.

RENAL CELL CARCINOMA

Renal cell carcinoma (RCC) was first described in 1884 by Paul Albert Grawitz (1850–1932), a German pathologist. He believed that it developed in cells surrounding the kidney. RCC actually starts in the cells that line the tubes of nephrons. RCC is usually found in only one kidney, but can form in both kidneys at the same time. Ninety percent of all adult kidney cancers are RCC.

Most renal cell carcinomas start from a new gene mutation in the person who develops the RCC. Some, however, occur in people who inherit a mutated gene from a parent or both parents. This is especially true if a person has family members with von Hippel-Lindau syndrome. People who have this syndrome can develop tumors in several places in their bodies, including their kidneys. The gene mutation that leads to renal cell carcinoma was first recognized when scientists were looking at the genetic makeup of people with von Hippel-Lindau syndrome. As a result, it is called the VHL gene.

TRANSITIONAL CELL CARCINOMA

Transitional cell carcinoma (TCC) starts in cells that line the pelvis of the kidney. TCC of the renal pelvis is more closely related to cancers

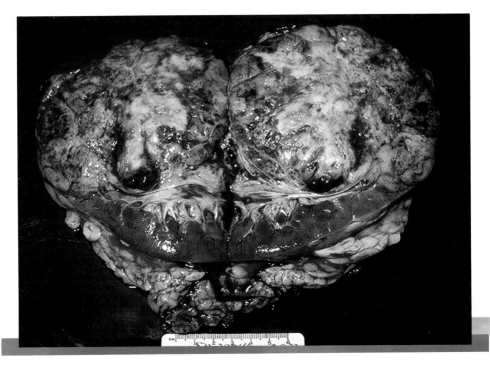

A large renal cell carcinoma (the yellow mass in the upper two-thirds of this photograph) almost completely replaces normal renal tissue in this bisected kidney.

that start in the urinary bladder than they are to renal cell carcinomas. Although they are diagnosed in the same way as renal cell carcinomas, TCCs are treated differently. TCC makes up 5 to 9 percent of adult kidney cancers.

RENAL SARCOMAS

Renal sarcomas, which make up 1 percent of adult kidney cancers, arise in connective tissues of the kidney or in its blood vessels. They can be found anywhere in the kidney. They usually occur in adults who are thirty to fifty years of age, rather than in older adults.

German pathologist Carl Max Wilhelm Wilms (1867–1918) thoroughly described kidney cancer in children in the late 1890s. Because of his studies, most childhood kidney cancers are today called Wilms tumors.

CHILDHOOD KIDNEY CANCERS

Carl Max Wilhelm Wilms (1867–1918) was a German pathologist and surgeon who studied childhood kidney cancer. He proposed that these cancers started while a child was still unborn. Because of the pioneering work that he did, the most common type of childhood kidney cancer was named Wilms tumor. Doctors now know that renal tissue in a very early embryo is made up of primitive cells that don't have a specific function. As an embryo develops, the cells mature and organize into normal kidney structures. Sometimes clumps of cells don't mature. They remain in their early primitive form even after a child is born. If they begin to multiply after birth, they may form a Wilms tumor. Ninety-five percent of children with kidney cancer have Wilms tumors.

Wilms tumors can occur anywhere in the kidney. More than one can occur in the same kidney. A few children will have them in both kidneys at the same time, which makes them much harder to treat. Like RCC, most Wilms tumors arise spontaneously (meaning that they are not inherited). There are, however, several genetic syndromes that include Wilms tumors as part of the syndrome.

Mesoblastic nephromas, clear cell sarcomas, and rhabdoid tumors of the kidney are the other types of childhood kidney cancers. They are generally found in very young children and are much harder to cure.

A Scavenger Hunt: Diagnosing Kidney Cancer

The scavenger hunt to diagnose kidney cancer follows the same rules as any scavenger hunt. A team consisting of a person who may or may not have kidney cancer and the doctor caring for that person starts the hunt with an initial set of clues.

Symptoms of Kidney Cancer: The First Clues

Most people go to the doctor because they notice a change in the way they feel or the way their bodies are functioning. These changes are called symptoms. Symptoms provide the first clues in this medical scavenger hunt. The three symptoms most commonly associated with kidney cancer are blood in the urine, pain in the lower back and side, and the presence of a lump that can be felt in the abdomen. Only 15 to 20 percent of people with kidney cancer have all of these symptoms. Symptoms as nonspecific as fever, weight loss, and tiredness are the ones that cause many people with kidney cancer to see their doctors.

Risk Factors for Kidney Cancer: The Second Set of Clues

Scientists have identified a series of factors that they believe increases an adult's risk for developing kidney cancer. A doctor will question a

A physician begins a "medical scavenger hunt" by taking a medical history from a patient. The symptoms described by the patient are the first clues used by the doctor to make a diagnosis.

person about these to seek additional clues for the scavenger hunt. The more risk factors a person has, the more likely the person is to have kidney cancer. The most significant risk factors for developing kidney cancers include the following:

— **Age.** Kidney cancer is diagnosed most often in people over the age of sixty.

— **Male sex.** Men are twice as likely as women to develop kidney cancer.

— **Smoking.** Cigarette smoke contains as many as forty-three substances that can cause cancer (known as carcinogens). When a person smokes, carcinogens in cigarette smoke are taken into the lungs. They are then absorbed into the blood to be carried throughout the body. Because the body's entire blood supply circulates through the kidneys several times each day, the cells that line the tubes of the nephrons and the cells lining the renal pelvis are constantly exposed to these carcinogens.

— **Obesity.** Being obese increases a person's risk for developing kidney cancer. This may be due to hormonal imbalances in obese people. Obese people also have some impairment of their immune systems that may contribute to the development of cancer.

— **High blood pressure.** Researchers don't know why having high blood pressure increases a person's risk for developing kidney cancer.

— **Exposure to chemicals in the workplace.** The National Institutes of Health has identified 28 definite carcinogens, 27 probable carcinogens, and 113 possible carcinogens in workplaces in the United States. Asbestos, cadmium, and trichloroethylene, a

chemical that dissolves grease and other impurities, are the carcinogens most often associated with kidney cancers.

—— **Treatment for kidney failure.** People who undergo long-term
renal dialysis for kidney failure develop kidney cancers more
often than people not receiving dialysis. The cause for this is
not understood.

—— **Inherited disorders.** Von Hippel-Lindau syndrome is an inherited disorder in which people develop several kinds of tumors,
including RCC. Wilms tumors that generally occur in childhood are not thought to result from environmental exposures
like some adult kidney cancers. Children may, however, inherit
defective genes that cause the cancer.

LABORATORY AND IMAGING STUDIES: THE NEXT SET OF CLUES

If a person's symptoms and risk factors suggest that he or she has kidney cancer, a third set of clues is sought. A doctor orders laboratory and
imaging tests to get specific information. A laboratory test that looks
for blood in a person's urine is always done when making the diagnosis
of kidney cancer. Tests done on a person's blood to see if the kidneys
are working properly are also important.

An abdominal ultrasound (US) scan is usually the first imaging study
ordered. This scan uses sound waves to make pictures of the kidneys.
The procedure is painless and very safe. Radiologists who interpret
ultrasounds can tell whether a kidney tumor is present or not and
whether it is likely to be cancer. Other imaging studies that may be
ordered include computerized tomography (CT) scans and magnetic
resonance imaging (MRI) scans. These studies are usually done not only
to evaluate the kidneys but also to look at the rest of the body. It is
important to know whether there is evidence of cancer anywhere else

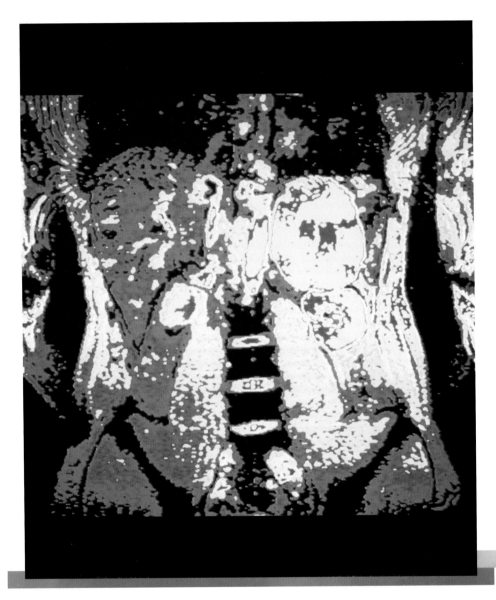

This colored magnetic resonance imaging (MRI) scan shows a large kidney cancer extending from the top of the patient's left kidney (the bright yellow mass on the right side of the picture).

in the body. Once the results of the laboratory and imaging tests have been evaluated, the final clue for the medical scavenger hunt is sought.

THE FINAL CLUE: A RENAL BIOPSY

Ultimately, the diagnosis of RCC requires that a piece of the tumor be removed and examined under a microscope. The procedure to remove the piece of tumor is called a biopsy. Kidney biopsies are usually done by inserting a very thin needle through a person's skin and into the tumor in the kidney. A doctor performs the biopsy under ultrasound or computed tomography guidance to make sure the needle is in the right place. Tumor cells are then removed and sent to a pathologist for evaluation.

Once the biopsy results have been evaluated, the goal of the medical scavenger hunt has been reached, and a diagnosis is made. If the person is found to have kidney cancer, the tumor is "staged" and a treatment plan is developed to try to cure him or her of the cancer. These steps will be discussed in the next chapter.

MYTHS AND FACTS

MYTH The cause of cancer is unknown.

FACT Scientists have learned that cancer occurs when the genes controlling cell growth, division, and death are damaged and mutate. These genes no longer direct the production of the appropriate protein, so cell division and growth go unchecked and cancers develop.

MYTH Smoking is a risk factor for developing lung cancer, but not kidney cancer.

FACT Smoking is a major risk factor in the development of adult kidney cancers, especially TCC. Carcinogens from cigarette smoke are absorbed through the lungs into the bloodstream and are carried to the kidneys. The cells lining the tubes of nephrons and the renal pelvis are exposed to these carcinogens over time and can be damaged by them.

MYTH Wilms tumors are just like renal cell carcinomas in adults and are treated the same way.

FACT Wilms tumors are quite different from renal cell carcinomas. They can occur anywhere in a child's kidneys and are usually quite large when they are diagnosed. They are treated not only with an operation, but also with chemotherapy and often with radiation therapy.

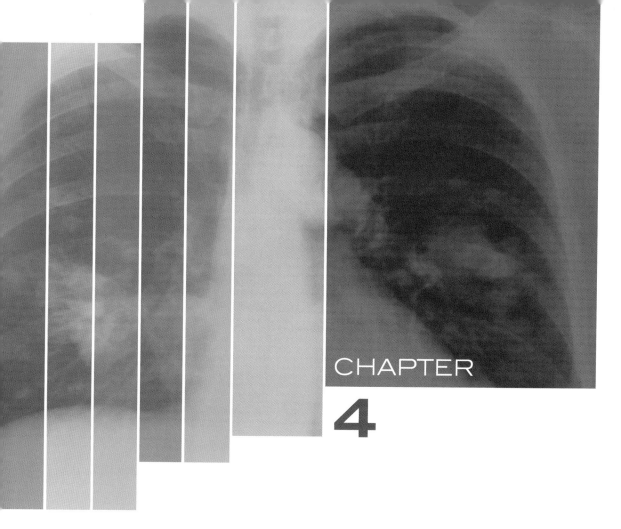

THE STAGING AND TREATMENT OF KIDNEY CANCER

Once the kidney cancer scavenger hunt has been completed and a diagnosis made, a person with kidney cancer wants to know how his or her cancer will be treated. Before providing that information, a doctor needs to know the stage of a person's cancer. What is a cancer stage? How is it determined? Why is it important?

STAGING KIDNEY CANCER

Staging is the process of determining how much cancer is present in a person's body and where it is located within the body. There are two

A pathologist microscopically examines the tissue from a kidney biopsy. The pathologist uses information from the examination to "stage" the cancer if it is present in the biopsy.

levels of staging. The first level is clinical staging, which is based on information that a doctor accumulates from a person's physical examination, laboratory and imaging tests, and kidney biopsy. It is the staging level that gives the most information about whether a person's cancer has spread (metastasized) to other organs or locations in the body.

The second level is called pathologic staging. After a person's affected kidney and the tissues surrounding it are removed, they are sent to a pathologist to be examined. By looking at the tissues under a microscope, the pathologist determines whether a cancer has spread outside the kidney, to other structures such as the adrenal gland, or to the lymph nodes. Information from clinical staging is then combined with what the pathologist has learned to produce the pathologic stage of the cancer.

The most common pathologic staging system is called the TNM system. It is based on how big the tumor is and whether it extends into the tissues around the kidney (T). The TNM system also looks to see if the tumor has spread into the lymph nodes (N) or to other areas of the body (M). A person with a very small kidney cancer that is contained within the kidney and who has no evidence of metastases has a T1N0M0 kidney cancer. If a person has a larger tumor that is found in two lymph nodes, but has no metastases, he or she has a T2N2M0 tumor.

Clinical staging is carried out before kidney cancers are treated. It is done to help a doctor plan the best treatment method for each patient. There are four clinical stages of renal cell carcinoma, as follows:

— **Stage I:** The tumor is less than 7 centimeters (2.76 in) in diameter and is found only in the kidney.
— **Stage II:** The tumor is greater than 7 centimeters (2.76 in) in diameter, but is still contained within the kidney.
— **Stage III:** The tumor extends beyond the kidney to surrounding fat or into the adrenal gland. It may also be present in the inferior vena cava.
— **Stage IV:** The cancer has spread to distant parts of the body.

Once the clinical stage of the kidney cancer has been determined, treatment options are discussed with the patient.

TREATING KIDNEY CANCER IN ADULTS
Renal cell carcinoma can't be killed by standard radiation therapy treatments or by chemotherapy drugs used for other types of cancer.

Doctors therefore recommend an operation called a radical nephrectomy to most patients with stages I, II, or III RCC. This operation involves the complete removal of the affected kidney, the fat surrounding the kidney, and any lymph nodes found in the area. The adrenal gland, which sits on top of the kidney, is also removed as is any tumor found within the inferior vena cava. Patients with stage IV (metastatic) disease may also undergo nephrectomy. Several studies have suggested that distant metastases may get smaller if the primary tumor in the kidney is removed.

The word "cure" is usually not used for people with cancers like RCC because the tumor can come back many years after it is initially treated. The term "survival rate" is used instead. The survival rate indicates the probability that a kidney cancer patient will live for five years after receiving a diagnosis of cancer. The five-year survival rates following radical nephrectomy for RCC parallel the clinical stage of the tumor.

Stage	Percentage of People Surviving for Five Years
I	90 percent
II	82 percent
III	64 percent
IV	23 percent

People with stages I and II RCC rarely have any treatment other than nephrectomies. They are watched closely and receive further treatment only if their cancers return. Patients with stages III and IV tumors are often entered into one of several clinical trials for kidney cancer. A clinical trial is a study that is conducted by scientists who are trying to find new ways to treat cancer.

A radical nephrectomy is also the best treatment for transitional cell carcinomas and renal sarcomas. People with stages I and II TCC have a

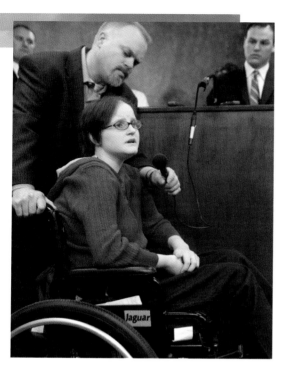

Eighteen-year-old Steffanie Collings, who was diagnosed with brain cancer and who supported insurance coverage for participants in clinical trials, is seen here at a press conference in Oklahoma City. If it is passed by Oklahoma's state legislature, "Steffanie's Law" will require health insurance providers in the state to pay for routine medical care for patients participating in clinical trials. Drug companies provide the medications that are studied in the trial.

90 percent five-year survival rate, but those with stage III and stage IV cancers have poorer outcomes. Their five-year survival rates drop to 10 percent to 15 percent with radical nephrectomy alone. Because TCC can be killed by some chemotherapy drugs, patients with stages III and IV TCC usually undergo chemotherapy after their nephrectomies. Renal sarcomas are difficult to treat. The overall five-year survival rate is 27 percent.

People who can't undergo nephrectomies because they are elderly or have coexisting health problems still have treatment options. These include the following:

— **Embolization therapy.** Cancers are very dependent on their blood supplies. Embolization therapy involves placing small metal coils or other devices into the renal artery. These block the blood flow into the kidney so that the tumor doesn't get oxygen or nutrients. The tumor, along with the kidney itself, shrinks, and eventually dies.

— **Cryoablation therapy.** This treatment method is effective in killing cancers that are less than 4 centimeters (1.6 inches) in size. Special needles called cryoprobes are placed into the tumor through small incisions in the skin. A very cold gas is passed through the needles into the tumor to freeze and kill it.

— **Radiofrequency ablation therapy.** This method involves placing a small electrode through the skin and into the kidney cancer. The electrode is then heated by a device that emits high-frequency energy (similar to microwaves). The heat kills tumor cells.

Each of these treatment methods carries its own risks. Fortunately, new treatment methods that can be used even in people who are very elderly are now being developed.

Staging and Treatment of Wilms Tumor

Wilms tumors are staged somewhat differently from RCC because the tumors are usually quite large when they are diagnosed. The clinical stages of Wilms tumors are as follows:

— **Stage I:** The cancer is found in only one kidney and can probably be removed with nephrectomy.

— **Stage II:** The cancer appears to be outside the kidney, but can probably be removed surgically.

— **Stage III:** The cancer is confined in the abdominal cavity, but is so big that it's unlikely that it can be removed without breaking it (tumor spillage).

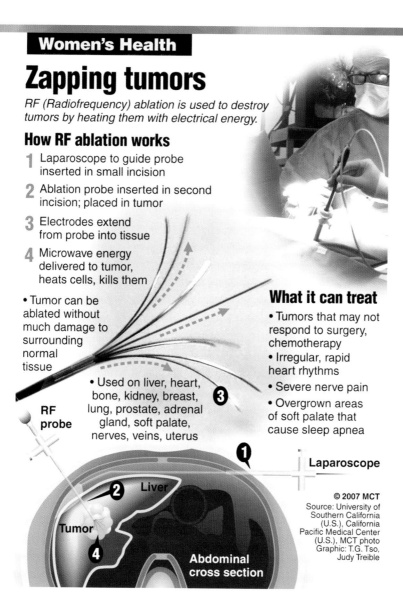

Women's Health

Zapping tumors

RF (Radiofrequency) ablation is used to destroy tumors by heating them with electrical energy.

How RF ablation works

1 Laparoscope to guide probe inserted in small incision

2 Ablation probe inserted in second incision; placed in tumor

3 Electrodes extend from probe into tissue

4 Microwave energy delivered to tumor, heats cells, kills them

• Tumor can be ablated without much damage to surrounding normal tissue

• Used on liver, heart, bone, kidney, breast, lung, prostate, adrenal gland, soft palate, nerves, veins, uterus

RF probe

What it can treat

• Tumors that may not respond to surgery, chemotherapy

• Irregular, rapid heart rhythms

• Severe nerve pain

• Overgrown areas of soft palate that cause sleep apnea

Laparoscope

Liver

Tumor

Abdominal cross section

© 2007 MCT
Source: University of Southern California (U.S.), California Pacific Medical Center (U.S.), MCT photo
Graphic: T.G. Tso, Judy Treible

Radiofrequency ablation therapy, as described here, is a treatment for kidney cancer that is available for some patients who cannot tolerate surgical removal of their cancers.

— Stage IV: The tumor has metastasized to other parts of the body.

— Stage V: There are tumors in both kidneys.

In the past, surgical removal of the entire kidney was considered the best treatment for children with stages I through IV Wilms tumors. Kidney-sparing operations in which some of the healthy kidney is left in place are now being used more frequently. Children with stage V cancers are treated with operations that try to preserve as much healthy tissue in each kidney as possible. Unlike RCC, Wilms tumors are sensitive to both radiation and chemotherapy drugs. Therefore, almost all children with higher stages of Wilms tumors are treated with all three methods. This combination of therapies has greatly increased survival. Overall, 90 percent of children with Wilms tumors are cured of their cancers.

Other childhood kidney cancers are not as successfully treated as Wilms tumors. Such tumors tend to be more undifferentiated (primitive) and may have metastasized by the time they are diagnosed. They are not very responsive to chemotherapy drugs. New treatment methods are being sought to improve the chances for survival in children who have these kinds of cancer.

COMPLEMENTARY AND ALTERNATIVE MEDICINE (CAM) TREATMENTS FOR KIDNEY CANCER

Complementary treatments are those that are used *along with* regular medical treatments. Complementary methods are not offered as cures for cancer. They are used to improve the well-being of a person who is undergoing standard methods of treatment. An example of a complementary treatment method is meditation. When people meditate, they visualize a beautiful place. Keeping that picture in mind, they concentrate on taking slow, deep breaths and relaxing. Meditating for as little as twenty minutes has been found to be helpful in reducing the stress experienced by people being treated for cancer. Complementary treatment methods recommended for children who have Wilms tumors include art therapy or play therapy to help them reduce stress and drinking peppermint tea to relieve nausea that may occur with standard treatment methods.

A MEDICAL MIRACLE

If something good happens that can't be explained by present knowledge, it is frequently called a miracle. Robert Langreth, a writer and editor at *Forbes* magazine, reports that a few people with advanced kidney cancer experience a medical miracle called spontaneous tumor regression. Their tumors get smaller and, in rare cases, disappear entirely without any type of treatment. Scientists believe that the immune systems of these people play a critical role in combating their cancers. The immune system is the body's defense against bacteria, viruses, and other harmful organisms. It also plays a role in helping prevent cancers. How it can be stimulated to control or kill existing cancers is being studied at many research institutes around the world. Two naturally occurring immune proteins, interleukin-2 and interferon-alpha, are presently being used to encourage a person's immune system to kill his or her kidney cancer. Only a few patients have shown improvement from the use of these immune proteins, though. New drugs that stimulate the immune system to fight cancers are now in clinical trials. Hopefully, they will soon be available to help create more medical miracles.

Alternative treatments are those used *instead of* standard methods of treatment. There are no known alternative treatments that cure people who have kidney cancers. Some dietary supplements, herbal products, and vitamins that are advertised as "cures" for cancer may actually be harmful to those being treated for cancer. They can interfere with the absorption of chemotherapy drugs and make them much less effective. They can also cause liver damage and harm a person's remaining kidney. People who are considering the use of such products should check with their doctors to make sure these agents won't interfere with other treatments they are receiving. The greatest danger of any of these treatments is that people who use them may miss a chance to be helped with standard forms of treatment.

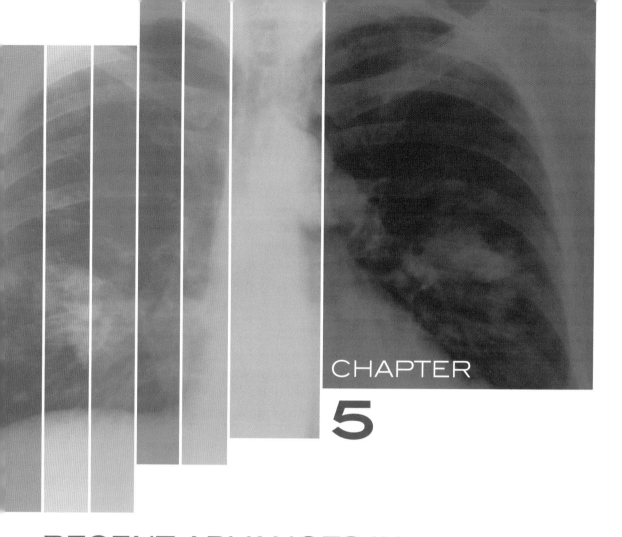

CHAPTER

5

RECENT ADVANCES IN CANCER TREATMENT

Targeted therapy, cancer vaccines, robots, and nanotechnology—all are providing new ways to treat kidney cancer. Older treatment methods such as radiofrequency ablation therapy are being modernized. New drugs are being developed that appear to be more effective in killing kidney cancer cells than those that are presently available. With each new development, survival statistics improve, and kidney cancer victims gain new hope. The following describes some of these new treatment methods.

TARGETED THERAPY

Standard drug therapy for cancer uses "poisons" that directly kill cancer cells. In the process, they also kill many healthy cells. Targeted therapy methods don't necessarily kill cancer cells themselves. They work by inactivating the abnormal proteins made by genes that have mutated. For example, several new drugs have been developed that specifically target the abnormal protein that causes massive numbers of new blood vessels to form around cancers.

The gene mutation that causes RCC is located on chromosome 3. It was discovered in 1993 when scientists were looking at the genomes of people who have von Hippel-Lindau syndrome. Scientists found that people with the syndrome who had RCC had changes in a gene on chromosome 3, while those without kidney cancer did not have the gene mutation. They named the gene the VHL gene, for von Hippel-Lindau. Once the gene was recognized, scientists looked at the same gene in people with RCC who did not have the syndrome. Many of them also had a VHL gene mutation.

The VHL gene contains the blueprint for the production of several proteins. One of these is a protein called vascular endothelial growth factor (VEGF). VEGF controls the development of new blood vessels around cells. The process is called angiogenesis. Angiogenesis is usually well controlled with just enough blood vessels being produced to support normal cell growth. When the VHL gene mutates, too much VEGF is produced. Huge numbers of new blood vessels develop around a cancer to deliver the oxygen and nutrients these rapidly growing cells must have.

Scientists have used their knowledge of VHL and VEGF to make drugs called angiogenesis inhibitors that prevent uncontrolled angiogenesis. They block the abnormal VEGF protein so that new blood

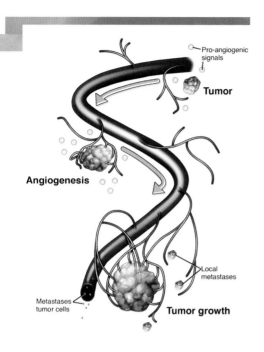

Angiogenesis is the development of blood vessels to carry oxygen and nutrients to growing tissues. Drugs that stop angiogenesis can kill cancers by preventing the growth of new blood vessels.

vessels do not form around kidney cancers. As a result, the tumors don't get enough oxygen and nutrients to grow or divide rapidly. Angiogenesis inhibitors that are currently available, unfortunately, do not cure people with RCC. They have been shown to prolong the lives of people with advanced RCC by up to two years, though. It is hoped that drugs that are now being developed to target angiogenesis will be even more effective and will offer the hope of a cure for advanced RCC.

CANCER VACCINES

Each winter, people in the United States receive vaccinations to protect them from the viruses that cause influenza (flu). People are injected with a vaccine that is made by suspending dead virus particles in a liquid. The immune systems of people who are vaccinated recognize that the viral proteins in the vaccine are foreign invaders that don't belong in their bodies. To kill these foreign invaders, their immune systems build antibodies against the viruses. If people are later exposed to live viruses of the same type, they already have some antibodies circulating in their blood that can kill them, and they can make more of these protective antibodies very quickly. Scientists are now using the same principle to build cancer vaccines. They hope these vaccines will prevent patients who have had a cancer from developing the same cancer again at a later date.

Oncophage is a cancer vaccine that has been created to use against RCC. It is still in developmental stages and is being used in clinical trials to see if it works. After a person, whose RCC is localized in his or her kidney, has the kidney removed, a piece of the tumor is taken and sent to the manufacturer of the vaccine. A personalized vaccine is then made and sent back to the patient's physician. The vaccine is injected into the person in hopes that he or she will build antibodies against the cancer cells from which the vaccine was made. If a person's cancer comes back, it is hoped that circulating antibodies will attack the cancer and destroy it.

Robots Aid in Treating Kidney Cancer

Surgeons have traditionally treated kidney cancer with radical nephrectomies. Today, surgeons can remove most small kidney cancers using a kidney-sparing approach. The operation involves the use of the da Vinci robotic surgical system. Instead of standing at an operating table, the surgeon sits at a console full of controls and monitors. The robotic device has four arms. One arm holds a camera, and the other three hold miniaturized surgical instruments. The camera and instruments are inserted into the patient's body through small cuts in the skin. Once in place, the arms are controlled by the surgeon's hand and finger movements using the console controls. The system allows the surgeon to see tissues and other structures very clearly and operate more

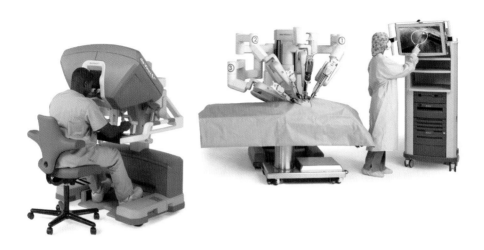

The robotic arms of the da Vinci surgical system (center) *are controlled by the surgeon, who sits at the console of the system* (left).

skillfully than he or she could without the device. Cancers can be removed, while healthy parts of the kidney are spared. The use of this system is especially important for people with cancer in both kidneys. Another advantage of the procedure is that patients recover much more quickly from this less invasive operation than from traditional nephrectomies.

Nanotechnology in the Treatment of Kidney Cancer

Nanotechnology was initially developed to build very small parts for use in computers and other technical instruments. It is now being used to help treat kidney cancer.

THINKING SMALL—REALLY SMALL

It is almost impossible to think small enough to understand what a nanometer is. An article from the Materials Research Science and Engineering Center at the University of Wisconsin-Madison helps put the nanoscale in perspective.

Size in the Metric System	Visual Image
1 meter	The height of an average elementary school student
1 centimeter (1/100 meter)	The width of your small finger or the width of a sugar cube
1 millimeter (1/1000 meter)	The thickness of a dime
1 micron (1/1,000,000 meter)	A human hair is 40–50 microns in diameter. A red blood cell is 6–10 microns in diameter.
1 nanometer (1/1,000,000,000 meter)	A virus is 30–50 nanometers in length. The width of a molecule of DNA is 2.5 nanometers. An atom is 0.1 to 0.3 nanometers in width. A sheet of paper is 100,000 nanometers thick.

Shaquille O'Neal, a professional basketball star, is 7 feet, 1 inch (2.1 meters) tall. Translated into nanometers, he is 2,160,000,000 nanometers tall.

Donald Tomalia is the scientific director of the Biologic Nanotechnology Center at the University of Michigan in Ann Arbor. Working with Dr. James Baker, the founder of the center, he has developed a nanotool called a dendrimer. This is a structure with many branches that looks like a small bush or tree. Dendrimers are thousands of times smaller than a cell in the human body. Because dendrimers have so many branches, they, like a toolbox, can carry a lot of "tools" into a body cell. These tools can be used to repair the cell, or in the case of a cancer cell, destroy it.

One of the reasons renal cell carcinomas cannot be successfully treated with standard chemotherapy drugs is that their cells are relatively insensitive to the drugs. It takes so much of a drug to kill the cancer cells that many healthy cells are also killed. Scientists working with Tomalia have found a way to insert dendrimers into cancer cells and not into healthy cells. By attaching drugs that will kill the cancer cells onto dendrimers, concentrated doses of the drug can be delivered to cancer cells without harming healthy cells. There are many other cancer treatment methods using nanotechnology that are presently in experimental stages of development.

HELPING YOURSELF

It is far better to try to prevent people from getting cancer than to treat them once they have it. That's why doctors recommend the following five self-help measures to minimize the risk of developing kidney cancer:

— Don't smoke or use "smokeless" tobacco products.
— Try to maintain a healthy body weight.
— Keep your blood pressure under good control.
— Protect yourself against toxic substances to which you may be exposed.

Eating a balanced diet not only helps people maintain a healthy weight, but also enhances the functioning of their immune system. Both are important in minimizing the risk of developing cancer.

Enhance your immune system by eating a well-rounded diet, getting plenty of sleep and exercise, and learning to deal with stress effectively.

CONCLUSION

Nearly fifty years ago, the only successful treatment for kidney cancer was a radical nephrectomy. People with small cancers, which could be completely removed with the operation, did well. Those with a more advanced case of the disease died. People with advanced kidney cancer are the ones who are getting the most benefit from new methods of cancer treatment today. It is probable that the most successful treatment methods of the future will be individualized. Cancer will be treated by drugs or procedures specifically designed for each person with cancer. The outlook for people who have kidney cancer is brighter today than it was yesterday because of advances in science and medicine. The future promises an even brighter outlook.

TEN GREAT QUESTIONS
TO ASK YOUR DOCTOR

1. What is kidney cancer?

2. What symptoms suggest that a person may have kidney cancer?

3. How are kidney cancers diagnosed?

4. What treatment options are there for kidney cancer?

5. What is a clinical trial?

6. Can kidney cancers be cured?

7. How often do kidney cancers recur?

8. Do children get kidney cancers?

9. Why do people who smoke get kidney cancer more often than those who don't smoke?

10. What's the association between obesity and kidney cancer?

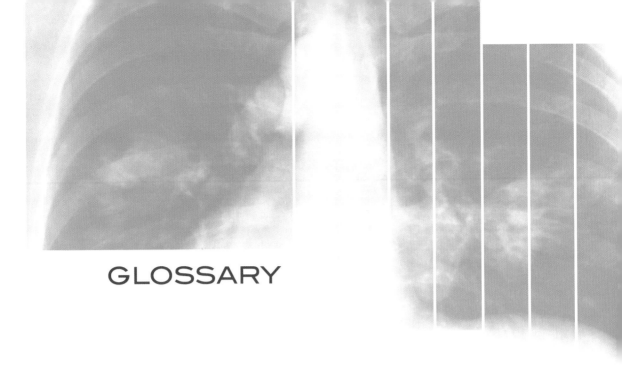

GLOSSARY

angiogenesis The production of blood vessels.

asbestos A mineral that occurs in fibrous masses. It is often used in insulation, roofing material, and fireproof curtains. It is a known carcinogen.

bone marrow The soft spongy material in the center of many bones that makes blood cells.

cadmium A white, metallic element used in many manufacturing processes. Some forms of cadmium are carcinogenic.

carcinogen A substance that will cause the mutation of a gene that leads to the formation of a cancer.

carcinoma A type of cancer that forms from epithelial cells.

computerized tomography (CT) scan A special imaging technique using X-rays in which detailed pictures of internal body structures can be made from many different angles.

electrode An instrument with a point from which an electric current can be directed into a body part.

enzyme An organic compound, frequently a protein, that causes an action or process to occur or speeds up a reaction.

genome A person's entire genetic composition.

hormone A chemical substance produced in one part of the body that, when transported to another part of the body, causes some type of action or process to occur.

ion An element that has a positive or negative electrical charge. Sodium, for instance, has a positive charge and will combine with chloride, which has a negative charge, to form sodium chloride (salt).

magnetic resonance imaging (MRI) scan An imaging procedure that uses strong magnetic fields to make detailed pictures of internal body structures.

mutate To change; to alter in form or function.

naturalist A person who is very interested in the natural sciences, especially those dealing with plants and animals.

phosphorus A nonmetallic element whose atomic number is 15. It is a component of bones and other body parts and is part of a DNA nucleotide.

physiologist A scientist who studies the function of organs or other structures of animals and plants.

probability The likelihood that an event or occurrence will happen.

renal dialysis The process of removing waste materials and extra body water directly from the blood of a person who has renal failure. The process involves circulating a person's blood through a dialysis machine.

renal transplant The transfer of a kidney from a donor to a person whose own kidneys no longer function. This is one of the most common types of organ transplants done in the United States.

sarcoma Tumors that arise from nonepithelial cells. They are the cancers found in connective tissue, lymphoid tissue, blood vessels, and bones.

spontaneous Not planned.

syndrome A set of symptoms that occur together. For instance, a sore throat, a drippy nose, and a cough make up a syndrome frequently associated with the common cold.

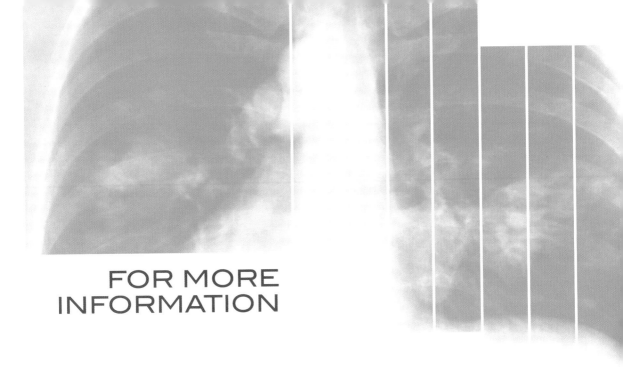

FOR MORE
INFORMATION

Kidney Cancer Association
1234 Sherman Avenue, Suite 203
Evanston, IL 60202
(800) 850-9132
Web site: http://kidneycancer.org.
This association funds research, educates families and physicians, and
serves as an advocate on behalf of patients.

Kidney Cancer Canada
880 Atwater Avenue
Mississauga, ON L5E 1M1
Canada
(519) 620-7241
Web site: http://www.kidneycancercanada.ca
Kidney Cancer Canada is a patient-led support and advocacy organiza-
tion. Its mission is to increase awareness about kidney cancer and
provide timely information to patients and caregivers facing a diagnosis of kidney cancer.

Kidney Foundation of Canada
300-5165 Sherbrooke Street West
Montreal, QC H4A 1T6
Canada
(541) 369-4806
Web site: http://www.kidney.ca
This national health charity is committed to kidney health and improv-
ing life for all people living with kidney disease.

National Cancer Institute
6116 Executive Boulevard, MSC 8322, Room 3036A
Bethesda, MD 20892-8322
(301) 435-3848
Web site: http://www.cancer.gov
The National Cancer Institute in the U.S. government's primary source
for cancer information, education, and research.

National Kidney Foundation
30 East 33rd Street
New York, NY 10016
(800) 622-9010
Web site: http://www.kidney.org
This foundation is dedicated to preventing kidney and urinary tract
disease and improving the health and well-being of individuals.

WEB SITES

Due to the changing nature of Internet links, Rosen Publishing has
developed an online list of Web sites related to the subject of this book.
This site is updated regularly. Please use this link to access the list:

http://www.rosenlinks.com/cms/kidn

FOR FURTHER READING

Bakewell, Lisa, and Karen Bellenir, eds. *Cancer Information for Teens: Health Tips About Cancer Awareness, Prevention, Diagnosis and Treatment* (Teen Health). 2nd ed. Detroit, MI: Omnigraphics, 2009.

Campbell, Stephen. *100 Questions and Answers About Kidney Cancer.* Sudbury, MA: Jones and Bartlett Publishing, 2009.

Keene, Maureen. *What to Eat If You Have Cancer: Healing Foods That Boost Your Immune System.* Rev ed. New York, NY: McGraw-Hill, 2007.

Keene, Nancy, Kathy Ruccione, and Wendy Hobbie. *Childhood Cancer Survivors: A Practical Guide to Your Future.* 2nd ed. Bellingham, WA: Childhood Cancer Guides, 2006.

Martin, Kim. *H Is for Hairy Fairy: An Alphabet of Encouragement and Insight for Kids (and Kids at Heart) with Cancer.* Bloomington, MN: Trafford Publishing, 2005.

Omoto, Charlotte, and Paul Lurquin. *Genes and DNA: A Beginner's Guide to Genetics and Its Application.* New York, NY: Columbia University Press, 2004.

Stille, Darlene. *Genetics: A Living Blueprint* (Exploring Science: Life Science Series). Mankato, MN: Compass Point Books, 2006.

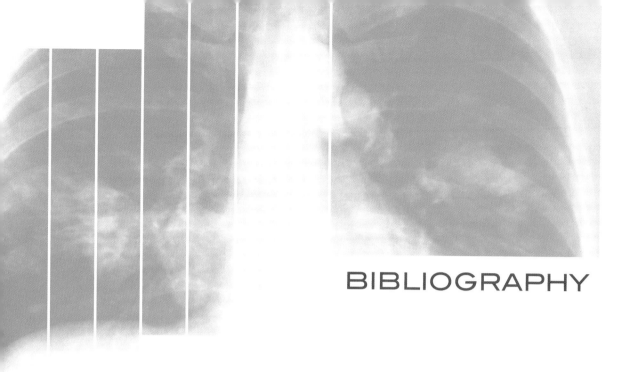

American Cancer Society. "Complementary and Alternative Methods for Cancer Management." June 11, 2009. Retrieved February 4, 2010 (http://www.cancer.org/docroot/ETO/content/ETO_5_1_Introduction.asp).

American Cancer Society. "The History of Cancer." Retrieved January 29, 2010 (http://www.cancer.org/docroot/cri/content/cri_2_6x_the_history_of_cancer_72.asp).

American Cancer Society. "What Is Kidney Cancer (Adult)-Renal Cell Carcinoma?" May 14, 2009. Retrieved January 26, 2010 (http://www.cancer.org/docroot/cri/content/cri_2_4_1x_what_is_kidney_cancer).

American Joint Committee on Cancer. "What Is Cancer Staging?" February 11, 2010. Retrieved February 18, 2010 (http://www.cancerstaging.org /mission/whatis.html).

Antigenics. "What Is Oncophage?" Retrieved February 4, 2010 (http://www.kidneycancervaccine.com/oncophage.html).

Cendron, Marc. "Wilms' Tumor." Emedicine, May 5, 2009. Retrieved January 26, 2010 (http://emedicine.medscape.com/article/989398-overview).

Columbia Urology. "Robotic Surgery for Kidney Cancer." Columbia University Medical Center. Retrieved January 26, 2010 (http://columbiaurology.org/specialties/roboticsurgery/kidney-cancer.html).

Fauci, Anthony, ed. *Harrison's Principles of Internal Medicine.* 14th ed. New York, NY: McGraw-Hill, 1998.

Freudenrich, Craig. "How DNA Works." HowStuffWorks. Retrieved February 11, 2010 (http://science.howstuffworks.com/cellular-microscopic-biology/dna.html).

Freudenrich, Craig. "How Your Kidneys Work." HowStuffWorks. Retrieved January 26, 2010 (http://health.howstuffworks.com/kidney.html).

HealthDay. "Obesity Tied to Common Kidney Cancer." January 22, 2010. Retrieved January 26, 2010 (http://www.businessweek.com/lifestyle/content/healthday/635042.html).

Kidney Cancer Association. "Therapies for Advanced Kidney Cancer." December 14, 2009. Retrieved January 27, 2010 (http://www.kidneycancer.org/knowledge/learn/therapies-for-advanced-kidney-cancer).

Langreth, Robert. "Cancer Miracles." *Forbes,* March 2, 2009. Retrieved February 18, 2010 (http://www.forbes.com/forbes/2009/0302/074_cancer_miracles_2.html.

Lerner, Eric. "Nano Is Now at Michigan—and James Baker is Leading the Way." Medicine at Michigan, 2000. Retrieved February 7, 2010 (http://www.medicineatmichigan.org/magazine/2000/summer/nanonman/default.asp).

Mayo Clinic Staff. "Kidney Cancer." February 9, 2008. Retrieved January 25, 2009 (http://www.mayoclinic.com/health/kidney-cancer/DS00360).

Mayo Clinic Staff. "Wilms' Tumor." September 5, 2009. Retrieved January 26, 2010 (http://www.mayoclinic.com/health/wilms-tumor/DS00436).

National Cancer Institute. "Cancer of the Kidney and Renal Pelvis."
    SEER Stat Fact Sheets, 2009. Retrieved February 8, 2010
    (http://seer.cancer.gov/statfacts/html/kidrp.html).
National Cancer Institute. "Kidney Cancer." National Institutes of
    Health. Retrieved February 17, 2010 (http://www.cancer.gov/
    cancertopics/types/kidney).
National Center for Complementary and Alternative Medicine.
    "Complementary and Alternative Medicine (CAM)." National
    Institutes of Health. Retrieved February 19, 2010 (http://www.
    cancer.gov/cancertopics/thinking-about-CAM).
National Human Genome Research Institute. "A Brief Guide to
    Genomics." National Institutes of Health, October 26, 2009.
    Retrieved January 29, 2010 (http://www.genome.gov/18016863).
Oregon Public Broadcasting. "Watson and Crick Describe Structure of
    DNA, 1953." Public Broadcasting System. Retrieved January 29,
    2010 (http://www.pbs.org/wgbh/aso/databank/entries/do53dn.html).
Palapattu, Ganesh, Blain Kristo, and Jacob Rajafer. "Paraneoplastic
    Syndromes in Urological Malignancy: The Many Faces of RCC."
    Reviews in Urology, Vol.4, No.4, Fall 2002, pp.163–170.
Sherwood, Chris. "How Does Kidney Cancer Start?" Retrieved
    February 4, 2010 (http://www.ehow.com/how-does_5393952_
    kidney-cancer-start.html).
University of Wisconsin-Madison. "Nanoscale." Materials Research
    Science and Engineering Center. Retrieved February 19, 2010
    (http://www.mrsec.wisc.edu/Edetc/nanoscale/index.html).
Wider, Jennifer. "Smoking Linked to Kidney Cancer." March 17, 2005.
    Retrieved January 26, 2010 (http://www.drdonnica.com/
    display.asp?article=9004).

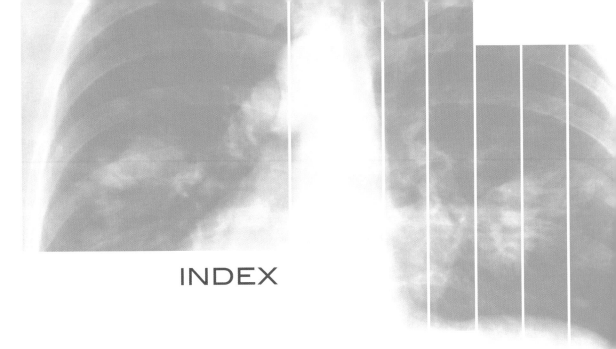

INDEX

ABOUT THE AUTHOR

Linda Bickerstaff is a retired general and peripheral vascular surgeon. She assisted urologists in doing several radical nephrectomies while still in practice. She was encouraged, while writing this book, to learn of new methods for treating kidney cancers. She has two friends with renal cell carcinoma who will hopefully benefit from them. Bickerstaff has written several books, including *Frequently Asked Questions About Concussions*, *Cocaine: Coke and the War on Drugs*, and *Violence Against Women: Public Health and Human Rights*.

PHOTO CREDITS

Cover, p. 1 © Science Photo Library/CMSP; cover (top), pp. 4–5 (bottom) Punchstock; back cover, pp. 3, 7, 14, 24, 35, 45, 54, 56, 58, 59, 62 National Cancer Institute; pp. 5, 39 © AP Images; p. 8 © Topham/ The Image Works; p. 8 (inset) http://ihm.nlm.nih.gov/images/B12562; p. 11 pttmedical/Newscom.com; p. 15 SSPL/Getty Images; p. 17 © Science Photo Library/CMSP; p. 19 http://en.wikipedia.org/wiki/ Edwin_Smith_Papyrus; p. 22 http://images.nigms.nih.gov; p. 26 Dr. Edwin P. Ewing, Jr./CDC; p. 27 http://ihm.nlm.nih.gov; p. 29 UpperCut Images/Getty Images; p. 32 © CNRI/Photo Researchers, Inc.; pp. 36, 52 Shutterstock.com; p. 41 Newscom.com; p. 47 © www.istockphoto.com/Claude Dagenais; p. 49 © 2010 Intuitive Surgical, Inc.

Designer: Evelyn Horovicz; Editor: Kathy Kuhtz Campbell; Photo Researcher: Amy Feinberg